NATIONAL STRATEGY FOR

COMBATING
TERRORISM

SEPTEMBER 2006

Table of Contents

Overview of America's National Strategy for Combating Terrorism

America is at war with a transnational terrorist movement fueled by a radical ideology of hatred, oppression, and murder. Our National Strategy for Combating Terrorism, first published in February 2003, recognizes that we are at war and that protecting and defending the Homeland, the American people, and their livelihoods remains our first and most solemn obligation.

Our strategy also recognizes that the War on Terror is a different kind of war. From the beginning, it has been both a battle of arms and a battle of ideas. Not only do we fight our terrorist enemies on the battlefield, we promote freedom and human dignity as alternatives to the terrorists' perverse vision of oppression and totalitarian rule. The paradigm for combating terrorism now involves the application of all elements of our national power and influence. Not only do we employ military power, we use diplomatic, financial, intelligence, and law enforcement activities to protect the Homeland and extend our defenses, disrupt terrorist operations, and deprive our enemies of what they need to operate and survive. We have broken old orthodoxies that once confined our counterterrorism efforts primarily to the criminal justice domain.

This updated strategy sets the course for winning the War on Terror. It builds directly from the National Security Strategy issued in March 2006 as well as the February 2003 National Strategy for Combating Terrorism, and incorporates our increased understanding of the enemy. From the beginning, we understood that the War on Terror involved more than simply finding and bringing to justice those who had planned and executed the terrorist attacks on September 11, 2001. Our strategy involved destroying the larger al-Qaida network and also confronting the radical ideology that inspired others to join or support the terrorist movement. Since 9/11, we have made substantial progress in degrading the al-Qaida network, killing or capturing key lieutenants, eliminating safehavens, and disrupting existing lines of support. Through the freedom agenda, we also have promoted the best long-term answer to al-Qaida's agenda: the freedom and dignity that comes when human liberty is protected by effective democratic institutions.

In response to our efforts, the terrorists have adjusted, and so we must continue to refine our strategy to meet the evolving threat. Today, we face a global terrorist movement and must confront the radical ideology that justifies the use of violence against innocents in the name of religion. As laid out in this strategy, to win the War on Terror, we will:

- Advance effective democracies as the long-term antidote to the ideology of terrorism;

- Prevent attacks by terrorist networks;

- Deny weapons of mass destruction to rogue states and terrorist allies who seek to use them;

- Deny terrorists the support and sanctuary of rogue states;

- Deny terrorists control of any nation they would use as a base and launching pad for terror; and

- Lay the foundations and build the institutions and structures we need to carry the fight forward against terror and help ensure our ultimate success.

Today's Realities in the War on Terror

The terrorist attacks of September 11, 2001, were acts of war against the United States, peaceful people throughout the world, and the very principles of liberty and human dignity. The United States, together with our Coalition partners, has fought back and will win this war. We will hold the perpetrators accountable and work to prevent the recurrence of similar atrocities on any scale – whether at home or abroad. The War on Terror extends beyond the current armed conflict that arose out of the attacks of September 11, 2001, and embraces all facets of continuing U.S. efforts to bring an end to the scourge of terrorism. Ultimately, we will win the long war to defeat the terrorists and their murderous ideology.

Successes

- We have deprived al-Qaida of safehaven in Afghanistan and helped a democratic government to rise in its place. Once a terrorist sanctuary ruled by the repressive Taliban regime, Afghanistan is now a full partner in the War on Terror.

- A multinational coalition joined by the Iraqis is aggressively prosecuting the war against the terrorists in Iraq. Together, we are working to secure a united, stable, and democratic Iraq, now a new War on Terror ally in the heart of the Middle East.

- We have significantly degraded the al-Qaida network. Most of those in the al-Qaida network responsible for the September 11 attacks, including the plot's mastermind Khalid Shaykh Muhammad, have been captured or killed. We also have killed other key al-Qaida members, such as Abu Musab al-Zarqawi, the group's operational commander in Iraq who led a campaign of terror that took the lives of countless American forces and innocent Iraqis.

- We have led an unprecedented international campaign to combat terrorist financing that has made it harder, costlier, and riskier for al-Qaida and related terrorist groups to raise and move money.

- There is a broad and growing global consensus that the deliberate targeting of innocents is never justified by any calling or cause.

- Many nations have rallied to fight terrorism, with unprecedented cooperation on law enforcement, intelligence, military, and diplomatic activity.

- We have strengthened our ability to disrupt and help prevent future attacks in the Homeland by enhancing our counterterrorism architecture through the creation of the Department of Homeland Security, the Office of Director of National Intelligence, and the National Counterterrorism Center. Overall, the United States and our partners have disrupted several serious plots since September 11, including al-Qaida plots to attack inside the United States.

- Numerous countries that were part of the problem before September 11 are now increasingly becoming part of the solution – and this transformation has occurred without destabilizing friendly regimes in key regions.

- The Administration has worked with Congress to adopt, implement, and renew key reforms like the USA PATRIOT Act that promote our security while also protecting our fundamental liberties.

Yet while America is safer, we are not yet safe. The enemy remains determined, and we face serious challenges at home and abroad.

Challenges

- Terrorist networks today are more dispersed and less centralized. They are more reliant on smaller cells inspired by a common ideology and less directed by a central command structure.

- While the United States Government and its partners have thwarted many attacks, we have not been able to prevent them all. Terrorists have struck in many places throughout the world, from Bali to Beslan to Baghdad.

- While we have substantially improved our air, land, sea, and border security, our Homeland is not immune from attack.

- Terrorists have declared their intention to acquire and use weapons of mass destruction (WMD) to inflict even more catastrophic attacks against the United States, our allies, partners, and other interests around the world.

- Some states, such as Syria and Iran, continue to harbor terrorists at home and sponsor terrorist activity abroad.

- The ongoing fight for freedom in Iraq has been twisted by terrorist propaganda as a rallying cry.

- Increasingly sophisticated use of the Internet and media has enabled our terrorist enemies to communicate, recruit, train, rally support, proselytize, and spread their propaganda without risking personal contact.

Today's Terrorist Enemy

The United States and our partners continue to pursue a significantly degraded but still dangerous al-Qaida network. Yet the enemy we face today in the War on Terror is not the same enemy we faced on September 11. Our effective counterterrorist efforts, in part, have forced the terrorists to evolve and modify their ways of doing business. Our understanding of the enemy has evolved as well. Today, the principal terrorist enemy confronting the United States is a transnational movement of extremist organizations, networks, and individuals – and their state and non-state supporters – which have in common that they exploit Islam and use terrorism for ideological ends.

This transnational movement is not monolithic. Although al-Qaida functions as the movement's vanguard and remains, along with its affiliate groups and those inspired by them, the most dangerous present manifestation of the enemy, the movement is not controlled by any single individual, group, or state. What unites the movement is a common vision, a common set of ideas about the nature and destiny of the world, and a common goal of ushering in totalitarian rule. What unites the movement is the ideology of oppression, violence, and hate.

Our terrorist enemies exploit Islam to serve a violent political vision. Fueled by a radical ideology and a false belief that the United States is the cause of most problems affecting Muslims today, our enemies seek to expel Western power and influence from the Muslim world and establish regimes that rule according to a violent and intolerant distortion of Islam. As illustrated by Taliban-ruled Afghanistan, such regimes would deny all political and religious freedoms and serve as sanctuaries for extremists to launch additional attacks against not only the United States, its allies and partners, but the Muslim world itself. Some among the enemy, particularly al-Qaida, harbor even greater territorial and geopolitical ambitions and aim to establish a single, pan-Islamic, totalitarian regime that stretches from Spain to Southeast Asia.

This enemy movement seeks to create and exploit a division between the Muslim and non-Muslim world and within the Muslim world itself. The terrorists distort the idea of jihad into a call for violence and murder against those they regard as apostates or unbelievers, including all those who disagree with them. Most of the terrorist attacks since September 11 have occurred in Muslim countries – and most of the victims have been Muslims.

In addition to this principal enemy, a host of other groups and individuals also use terror and violence against innocent civilians to pursue their political objectives. Though their motives and goals may be different, and often include secular and more narrow territorial aims, they threaten our interests and those of our partners as they attempt to overthrow civil order and replace freedom with conflict and intolerance. Their terrorist tactics ensure that they are enemies of humanity regardless of their goals and no matter where they operate.

For our terrorist enemies, violence is not only justified, it is necessary and even glorified – judged the only means to achieve a world vision darkened by hate, fear, and oppression. They use suicide bombings, beheadings, and other atrocities against innocent people as a means to promote their creed. Our enemy's demonstrated indifference to human life and desire to inflict catastrophic damage on the United States and its friends and allies around the world have fueled their desire for weapons of mass destruction. We cannot permit the world's most dangerous terrorists and their regime sponsors to threaten us with the world's most destructive weapons.

For the enemy, there is no peaceful coexistence with those who do not subscribe to their distorted and violent view of the world. They accept no dissent and tolerate no alternative points of view. Ultimately, the terrorist enemy we face threatens global peace, international security and prosperity, the rising tide of democracy, and the right of all people to live without fear of indiscriminate violence.

Strategic Vision for the War on Terror

From the beginning, the War on Terror has been both a battle of arms and a battle of ideas – a fight against the terrorists and their murderous ideology. In the short run, the fight involves the application of all instruments of national power and influence to kill or capture the terrorists; deny them safehaven and control of any nation; prevent them from gaining access to WMD; render potential terrorist targets less attractive by strengthening security; and cut off their sources of funding and other resources they need to operate and survive. In the long run, winning the War on Terror means winning the battle of ideas. Ideas can transform the embittered and disillusioned either into murderers willing to kill innocents, or into free peoples living harmoniously in a diverse society.

The battle of ideas helps to define the strategic intent of our National Strategy for Combating Terrorism. The United States will continue to lead an expansive international effort in pursuit of a two-pronged vision:

- The defeat of violent extremism as a threat to our way of life as a free and open society; and

- The creation of a global environment inhospitable to violent extremists and all who support them.

Strategy for Winning the War on Terror

Long-term approach: Advancing effective democracy

The long-term solution for winning the War on Terror is the advancement of freedom and human dignity through effective democracy. Elections are the most visible sign of a free society and can play a critical role in advancing effective democracy. But elections alone are not enough. Effective democracies honor and uphold basic human rights, including freedom of religion, conscience, speech, assembly, association, and press. They are responsive to their citizens, submitting to the will of the people. Effective democracies exercise effective sovereignty and maintain order within their own borders, address causes of conflict peacefully, protect independent and impartial systems of justice, punish crime, embrace the rule of law, and resist corruption. Effective democracies also limit the reach of government, protecting the institutions of civil society. In effective democracies, freedom is indivisible. They are the long-term antidote to the ideology of terrorism today. This is the battle of ideas.

To wage the battle of ideas effectively, we must recognize what does and does not give rise to terrorism:

- Terrorism is not the inevitable by-product of poverty. Many of the September 11 hijackers were from middle-class backgrounds, and many terrorist leaders, like bin Laden, are from privileged upbringings.

- Terrorism is not simply a result of hostility to U.S. policy in Iraq. The United States was attacked on September 11 and many years earlier, well before we toppled the Saddam Hussein regime. Moreover, countries that did not participate in Coalition efforts in Iraq have not been spared from terror attacks.

- Terrorism is not simply a result of Israeli-Palestinian issues. Al-Qaida plotting for the September 11 attacks began in the 1990s, during an active period in the peace process.

- Terrorism is not simply a response to our efforts to prevent terror attacks. The al-Qaida network targeted the United States long before the United States targeted al-Qaida. Indeed, the terrorists are emboldened more by perceptions of weakness than by demonstrations of resolve. Terrorists lure recruits by telling them that we are decadent, easily intimidated, and will retreat if attacked.

The terrorism we confront today springs from:

- *Political alienation.* Transnational terrorists are recruited from populations with no voice in their own government and see no legitimate way to promote change in their own country. Without a stake in the existing order, they are vulnerable to manipulation by those who advocate a perverse political vision based on violence and destruction.

- *Grievances that can be blamed on others.* The failures the terrorists feel and see are blamed both on others and on perceived injustices from the recent or sometimes distant past. The terrorists' rhetoric keeps wounds associated with this past fresh and raw, a potent motivation for revenge and terror.

- *Subcultures of conspiracy and misinformation.* Terrorists recruit more effectively from populations whose information about the world is contaminated by falsehoods and corrupted by conspiracy theories. The distortions keep alive grievances and filter out facts that would challenge popular prejudices and self-serving propaganda.

- *An ideology that justifies murder.* Terrorism ultimately depends upon the appeal of an ideology that excuses or even glorifies the deliberate killing of innocents. Islam has been twisted and made to serve an evil end, as in other times and places other religions have been similarly abused.

Defeating terrorism in the long run requires that each of these factors be addressed. Effective democracy provides a counter to each, diminishing the underlying conditions terrorists seek to exploit.

- In place of alienation, democracy offers an ownership stake in society, a chance to shape one's own future.

- In place of festering grievances, democracy offers the rule of law, the peaceful resolution of disputes, and the habits of advancing interests through compromise.

- In place of a culture of conspiracy and misinformation, democracy offers freedom of speech, independent media, and the marketplace of ideas, which can expose and discredit falsehoods, prejudices, and dishonest propaganda.

- In place of an ideology that justifies murder, democracy offers a respect for human dignity that abhors the deliberate targeting of innocent civilians.

Democracy is the antithesis of terrorist tyranny, which is why the terrorists denounce it and are willing to kill the innocent to stop it. Democracy is based on empowerment, while the terrorists' ideology is based on enslavement. Democracies expand the freedom of their citizens, while the terrorists seek to impose a single set of narrow beliefs. Democracy sees individuals as equal in worth and dignity, having an inherent potential to create, govern themselves, and exercise basic freedoms of speech and conscience. The terrorists see individuals as objects to be exploited, and then to be ruled and oppressed.

Democracies are not immune to terrorism. In some democracies, some ethnic or religious groups are unable or unwilling to grasp the benefits of freedom otherwise available in the society. Such groups can evidence the same alienation and despair that the transnational terrorists exploit in undemocratic states. This accounts for the emergence in democratic societies of homegrown terrorists – even among second- and third-generation citizens. Even in these cases, the long-term solution remains deepening the reach of democracy so that all citizens enjoy its benefits. We will continue to guard against the emergence of homegrown terrorists within our own Homeland as well.

The strategy to counter the lies behind the terrorists' ideology and deny them future recruits must empower the very people the terrorists most want to exploit: the faithful followers of Islam. We will continue to support political reforms that empower peaceful Muslims to practice and interpret their faith. We will work to undermine the ideological underpinnings of violent Islamic extremism and gain the support of non-violent Muslims around the world. The most vital work will be done within the Islamic world itself, and Jordan, Morocco, and Indonesia, among others, have begun to make important strides in this effort. Responsible Islamic leaders need to denounce an ideology that distorts and exploits Islam to justify the murder of innocent people and defiles a proud religion.

Many of the Muslim faith are already making this commitment at great personal risk. They realize they are a target of this ideology of terror. Everywhere we have joined in the fight against terrorism, Muslim allies have stood beside us, becoming partners in this vital cause. They know the stakes – the survival of their own liberty, the future of their own region, the justice and humanity of their own traditions – and the United States is proud to stand beside them. Not only will we continue to support the efforts of our Muslim partners overseas to reject violent extremism, we will continue to engage with and strengthen the efforts of Muslims within the United States as well. Through outreach programs and public diplomacy we will reveal the terrorists' violent extremist ideology for what it is – a form of totalitarianism following in the path of fascism and Nazism.

Over the short term: Four priorities of action

The advance of freedom, opportunity, and human dignity through democracy is the long-term solution to the transnational terror movement of today. To create the space and time for this long-term solution to take root, we are operating along four priorities of action in the short term.

Prevent attacks by terrorist networks. A government has no higher obligation than to protect the lives and livelihoods of its citizens. The hard core among our terrorist enemies cannot be reformed or deterred; they will be tracked down, captured, or killed. They will be cut off from the network of individuals, institutions, and other resources they depend on for support and that facilitate their activities. The network, in turn, will be deterred, disrupted, and disabled. Working with committed partners across the globe, we continue to use a broad range of tools at home and abroad to take the fight to the terrorists, deny them entry to the United States, hinder their movement across international borders, and establish protective measures to further reduce our vulnerability to attack.

- *Attack terrorists and their capacity to operate.* The United States and our partners continue to take active and effective measures against our primary terrorist enemies and certain other violent extremist groups that also pose a serious and continuing threat. We are attacking these terrorists and their capacity to operate effectively at home and abroad. Specifically, through the use of all elements of national power, we are denying or neutralizing what our terrorist enemies need to operate and survive:

  - *Leaders,* who provide the vision that followers strive to realize. They also offer the necessary direction, discipline, and motivation for accomplishing a given goal or task. Most terrorist organizations have a central figure who embodies the cause, in addition to several operational leaders and managers who provide guidance on a functional, regional, or local basis. The loss of a leader can degrade a group's cohesiveness and in some cases may trigger its collapse. Other terrorist groups adapt by promoting experienced cadre or decentralizing their command structures, making our challenge in neutralizing terrorist leaders even greater.

- *Foot soldiers*, which include the operatives, facilitators, and trainers in a terrorist network. They are the lifeblood of a terrorist group – they make it run. Technology and globalization have enhanced the ability of groups to recruit foot soldiers to their cause, including well-educated recruits. We and our partners will not only continue to capture and kill foot soldiers, but will work to halt the influx of recruits into terrorist organizations as well. Without a continuing supply of personnel to facilitate and carry out attacks, these groups ultimately will cease to operate.

- *Weapons,* or the tools of terrorists and the means by which they murder to advance their cause. Terrorists exploit many avenues to develop and acquire weapons, including through state sponsors, theft or capture, and black market purchases. Our enemies employ existing technology – explosives, small arms, missiles and other devices – in both conventional and unconventional ways to terrorize and achieve mass effects. They also use non-weapon technologies as weapons, such as the airplanes on September 11. Our greatest and gravest concern, however, is WMD in the hands of terrorists. Preventing their acquisition and the dire consequences of their use is a key priority of this strategy.

- *Funds*, which provide the fungible, easily transportable means to secure all other forms of material support necessary to the survival and operation of terrorist organizations. Our enemies raise funds through a variety of means, including soliciting contributions from supporters; operating businesses, NGOs, and charitable fronts; and engaging in criminal activity such as fraud, extortion, and kidnapping for ransom. They transfer funds through several mechanisms, including the formal banking system, wire transfers, debit or "smart" cards, cash couriers, and *hawalas*, which are alternative remittance systems based on trust. Effective disruption of funding sources and interdiction of transfer mechanisms can help our partners and us to starve terrorist networks of the material support they require.

- *Communications*, which allow terrorists the ability to receive, store, manipulate, and exchange information. The methods by which terrorists communicate are numerous and varied. Our enemies rely on couriers and face-to-face contacts with associates and tend to use what is accessible in their local areas as well as what they can afford. They also use today's technologies with increasing acumen and sophistication. This is especially true with the Internet, which they exploit to create and disseminate propaganda, recruit new members, raise funds and other material resources, provide instruction on weapons and tactics, and plan operations. Without a communications ability, terrorist groups cannot effectively organize operations, execute attacks, or spread their ideology. We and our partners will continue to target the communication nodes of our enemy.

- *Propaganda operations*, which are used by terrorists to justify violent action as well as inspire individuals to support or join the movement. The ability of terrorists to exploit the Internet and 24/7 worldwide media coverage allows them to bolster their prominence as well as feed a steady diet of radical ideology, twisted images, and conspiracy theories to potential recruits in all corners of the globe. Besides a global reach, these technologies allow terrorists to propagate their message quickly, often before an effective counter to terrorist messages can be coordinated and distributed. These are force multipliers for our enemy.

- ***Deny terrorists entry to the United States and disrupt their travel internationally.*** Denying our enemies the tools to travel internationally and across and within our borders significantly impedes their mobility and can inhibit their effectiveness. They rely on illicit networks to facilitate travel and often obtain false identification documents through theft or in-house forgery operations. We will continue to enhance the security of the American people through a layered system of protections along our borders, at our ports, on our roadways and railways, in our skies, and with our international partners. We will continue to develop and enhance security practices and technologies to reduce vulnerabilities in the dynamic transportation network, inhibit terrorists from crossing U.S. borders, and detect and prevent terrorist travel within the United States. Our efforts will include improving all aspects of aviation security; promoting secure travel and identity documents; disrupting travel facilitation networks; improving border security and visa screening; and building international capacity and improving international information exchange to secure travel and combat terrorist travel. Our National Strategy to Combat Terrorist Travel and our National Strategy for Maritime Security will help guide our efforts.

- ***Defend potential targets of attack.*** Our enemies are opportunistic, exploiting vulnerabilities and seeking alternatives to those targets with increased security measures. The targeting trend since at least September 11 has been away from hardened sites, such as official government facilities with formidable security, and toward softer targets – schools, restaurants, places of worship, and nodes of public transportation – where innocent civilians gather and which are not always well secured. Specific targets vary, but they tend to be symbolic and often selected because they will produce mass casualties, economic damage, or both.

  While it is impossible to protect completely all potential targets all the time, we can deter and disrupt attacks, as well as mitigate the effects of those that do occur, through strategic security improvements at sites both at home and overseas. Among our most important defensive efforts is the protection of critical infrastructures and key resources – sectors such as energy, food and agriculture, water, telecommunications, public health, transportation, the defense industrial base, government facilities, postal and shipping, the chemical industry, emergency services, monuments and icons, information technology, dams, commercial facilities, banking and finance, and nuclear reactors, materials, and waste. These are systems and assets so vital that their destruction or incapacitation would have a debilitating effect on the security of our Nation. We will also continue to protect various assets such as historical attractions or certain high-profile events whose destruction or attack would not necessarily debilitate our national security but could damage the morale and confidence of the American people. Beyond the Homeland, we will continue to protect and defend U.S. citizens, diplomatic missions, and military facilities overseas, as well as work with our partners to strengthen their ability to protect their populations and critical infrastructures.

Deny WMD to rogue states and terrorist allies who seek to use them. Weapons of mass destruction in the hands of terrorists is one of the gravest threats we face. We have taken aggressive efforts to deny terrorists access to WMD-related materials, equipment, and expertise, but we will enhance these activities through an integrated effort at all levels of government and with the private sector and our foreign partners to stay ahead of this dynamic and evolving threat. In July 2006, the United States and Russia launched the Global Initiative to Combat Nuclear Terrorism to establish an international framework to enhance cooperation, build capacity, and act to combat the global threat of nuclear terrorism. This initiative will help drive international focus and action to ensure the international community is doing everything possible to prevent nuclear weapons, materials, and knowledge from reaching the hands of terrorists.

With regard to our own efforts, our comprehensive approach for addressing WMD terrorism hinges on six objectives, and we will work across all objectives simultaneously to maximize our ability to eliminate the threat.

- *Determine terrorists' intentions, capabilities, and plans to develop or acquire WMD.* We need to understand and assess the credibility of threat reporting and provide technical assessments of terrorists' WMD capabilities.

- *Deny terrorists access to the materials, expertise, and other enabling capabilities required to develop WMD.* We have an aggressive, global approach to deny our enemies access to WMD-related materials (with a particular focus on weapons-usable fissile materials), fabrication expertise, methods of transport, sources of funds, and other capabilities that facilitate the execution of a WMD attack. In addition to building upon existing initiatives to secure materials, we are developing innovative approaches that blend classic counterproliferation, nonproliferation, and counterterrorism efforts.

- *Deter terrorists from employing WMD.* A new deterrence calculus combines the need to deter terrorists and supporters from contemplating a WMD attack and, failing that, to dissuade them from actually conducting an attack. Traditional threats may not work because terrorists show a wanton disregard for the lives of innocents and in some cases for their own lives. We require a range of deterrence strategies that are tailored to the situation and the adversary. We will make clear that terrorists and those who aid or sponsor a WMD attack would face the prospect of an overwhelming response to any use of such weapons. We will seek to dissuade attacks by improving our ability to mitigate the effects of a terrorist attack involving WMD – to limit or prevent large-scale casualties, economic disruption, or panic. Finally, we will ensure that our capacity to determine the source of any attack is well-known, and that our determination to respond overwhelmingly to any attack is never in doubt.

- *Detect and disrupt terrorists' attempted movement of WMD-related materials, weapons, and personnel.* We will expand our global capability for detecting illicit materials, weapons, and personnel transiting abroad or heading for the United States or U.S. interests overseas. We will use our global partnerships, international agreements, and ongoing border security and interdiction efforts. We also will continue to work with countries to enact and enforce strict penalties for WMD trafficking and other suspect WMD-related activities.

- *Prevent and respond to a WMD-related terrorist attack.* Once the possibility of a WMD attack against the United States has been detected, we will seek to contain, interdict, and eliminate the threat. We will continue to develop requisite capabilities to eliminate the possibility of a WMD operation and to prevent a possible follow-on attack. We will prepare ourselves for possible WMD incidents by developing capabilities to manage the range of consequences that may result from such an attack against the United States or our interests around the world.

- ***Define the nature and source of a terrorist-employed WMD device.*** Should a WMD terrorist attack occur, the rapid identification of the source and perpetrator of an attack will enable our response efforts and may be critical in disrupting follow-on attacks. We will develop the capability to assign responsibility for the intended or actual use of WMD via accurate attribution – the rapid fusion of technical forensic data with intelligence and law enforcement information.

Deny terrorists the support and sanctuary of rogue states. The United States and its allies and partners in the War on Terror make no distinction between those who commit acts of terror and those who support and harbor terrorists. Any government that chooses to be an ally of terror has chosen to be an enemy of freedom, justice, and peace. The world will hold those regimes to account. To break the bonds between rogue states and our terrorist enemies, we will work to disrupt the flow of resources from states to terrorists while simultaneously working to end state sponsorship of terrorism.

- ***End state sponsorship of terrorism.*** State sponsors are a critical resource for our terrorist enemies, often providing funds, weapons, training, safe passage, and sanctuary. Some of these countries have developed or have the capability to develop WMD and other destabilizing technologies that could fall into the hands of terrorists. The United States currently designates five state sponsors of terrorism: Iran, Syria, Sudan, North Korea, and Cuba. We will maintain sanctions against them and promote their international isolation until they end their support for terrorists, including the provision of sanctuary. To further isolate these regimes and persuade other states not to sponsor terror, we will use a range of tools and efforts to delegitimate terrorism as an instrument of statecraft. Any act of international terrorism, whether committed by a state or individual, is reprehensible, a threat to international peace and security, and should be unequivocally and uniformly rejected. Similarly, states that harbor and assist terrorists are as guilty as the terrorists, and they will be held to account.

Iran remains the most active state sponsor of international terrorism. Through its Islamic Revolutionary Guard Corps and Ministry of Intelligence and Security, the regime in Tehran plans terrorist operations and supports groups such as Lebanese Hizballah, Hamas, and Palestine Islamic Jihad (PIJ). Iran also remains unwilling to account for and bring to justice senior al-Qaida members it detained in 2003. Most troubling is the potential WMD-terrorism nexus that emanates from Tehran. Syria also is a significant state sponsor of terrorism and thus a priority for concern. The regime in Damascus supports and provides haven to Hizballah, Hamas, and PIJ. We will continue to stand with the people of Iran and Syria against the regimes that oppress them at home and sponsor terror abroad.

While Iranian and Syrian terrorist activities are especially worrisome, we are pressing all state sponsors to take the steps that are required to have state sponsorship designation rescinded. Each case is unique, and our approach to each will be tailored accordingly. Moreover, we never foreclose future membership in the coalition against tyranny and terror. The designation of Iraq as a state sponsor was rescinded in 2004 as it transitioned to democracy, ceased its terrorist support, and became an ally in the War on Terror. Similarly, the United States in June 2006 rescinded the designation of Libya, which has renounced terrorism and since September 11 has provided excellent cooperation to the United States and other members of the international community in response to the new global threats we face. Libya can serve as a model for states who wish to rejoin the community of nations by rejecting terror.

- ***Disrupt the flow of resources from rogue states to terrorists.*** Until we can eliminate state sponsorship of terror, we will disrupt and deny the flow of support from states to terrorists. We will continue to create and strengthen international will to interdict material support, akin to our efforts in the Proliferation Security Initiative – a global effort to stop shipments of WMD, their delivery systems, and related material. We will build international cooperation to financially isolate rogue states and their terrorist proxies. We also will continue to expose the vehicles and fronts that states use to support their terrorist surrogates.

Deny terrorists control of any nation they would use as a base and launching pad for terror. Our terrorist enemies are striving to claim a strategic country as a haven for terror. From this base, they could destabilize the Middle East and strike America and other free nations with ever-increasing violence. This we can never allow. Our enemies had established a sanctuary in Afghanistan prior to Operation Enduring Freedom, and today terrorists see Iraq as the central front of their fight against the United States. This is why success in helping the Afghan and Iraqi peoples forge effective democracies is vital. We will continue to prevent terrorists from exploiting ungoverned or under-governed areas as safehavens – secure spaces that allow our enemies to plan, organize, train, and prepare for operations. Ultimately, we will eliminate these havens altogether.

- ***Eliminate physical safehavens.*** Physical sanctuaries can stretch across an entire sovereign state, be limited to specific ungoverned or ill-governed areas in an otherwise functioning state, or cross national borders. In some cases the government wants to exercise greater effective sovereignty over its lands and maintain control within its borders but lacks the necessary capacity. We will strengthen the capacity of such War on Terror partners to reclaim full control of their territory through effective police, border, and other security forces as well as functioning systems of justice. To further counter terrorist exploitation of under-governed lands, we will promote effective economic development to help ensure long-term stability and prosperity. In failing states or states emerging from conflict, the risks are significant. Spoilers can take advantage of instability to create conditions terrorists can exploit. We will continue to work with foreign partners and international organizations to help prevent conflict and respond to state failure by building foreign capacity for peace operations, reconstruction, and stabilization so that countries in transition can reach a sustainable path to peace, democracy, and prosperity. Where physical havens cross national boundaries, we will continue to work with the affected countries to help establish effective cross-border control. Yet some countries will be reluctant to fulfill their sovereign responsibilities to combat terrorist-related activities within their borders. In addition to cooperation and sustained diplomacy, we will continue to partner with the international community to persuade states to meet their obligations to combat terrorism and deny safehaven under U.N. Security Council Resolution 1373.

Yet safehavens are not just limited to geographic territories. They also can be non-physical or virtual, existing within legal, cyber, and financial systems.

- *Legal safehavens.* Some legal systems lack adequate procedural, substantive, and international assistance laws that enable effective investigation, prosecution, and extradition of terrorists. Such gaps offer a haven in which terrorists and their organizations can operate free from fear of prosecution. In the United States we have developed a domestic legal system that supports effective investigation and prosecution of terrorist activities while preserving individual privacy, the First Amendment rights of association, religious freedom, free speech, and other civil rights. We will continue to work with foreign partners to build their legal capacity to investigate, prosecute, and assist in the foreign prosecution of the full range of terrorist activities – from provision of material support to conspiracy to operational planning to a completed act of terrorism.

- *Cyber safehavens.* The Internet provides an inexpensive, anonymous, geographically unbounded, and largely unregulated virtual haven for terrorists. Our enemies use the Internet to develop and disseminate propaganda, recruit new members, raise and transfer funds, train members on weapons use and tactics, and plan operations. Terrorist organizations can use virtual safehavens based anywhere in the world, regardless of where their members or operatives are located. Use of the Internet, however, creates opportunities for us to exploit. To counter terrorist use of the Internet as a virtual sanctuary, we will discredit terrorist propaganda by promoting truthful and peaceful messages. We will seek ultimately to deny the Internet to the terrorists as an effective safehaven for their propaganda, proselytizing, recruitment, fund-raising, training, and operational planning.

- *Financial safehavens.* Financial systems are used by terrorist organizations as a fiscal sanctuary in which to store and transfer the funds that support their survival and operations. Terrorist organizations use a variety of financial systems, including formal banking, wire transfers, debit and other stored value cards, online value storage and value transfer systems, the informal *hawala* system, and cash couriers. Terrorist organizations may be able to take advantage of such financial systems either as the result of willful complicity by financial institutions or as the result of poor oversight and monitoring practices. Domestically, we have hardened our financial systems against terrorist abuse by promulgating effective regulations, requiring financial institutions to report suspicious transactions, and building effective public/private partnerships. We will continue to work with foreign partners to ensure they develop and implement similar regulations, requirements, and partnerships with their financial institutions. We also will continue to use the domestic and international designation and targeted sanctions regimes provided by, among other mechanisms, Executive Order 13224, USA PATRIOT Act Section 311, and United Nations Security Council Resolution 1267 and subsequent resolutions. These tools identify and isolate those actors who form part of terrorist networks or facilitate their activities.

Institutionalizing Our Strategy for Long-term Success

The War on Terror will be a long war. Yet we have mobilized to win other long wars, and we can and will win this one. During the Cold War we created an array of domestic and international institutions and enduring partnerships to defeat the threat of communism. Today, we require similar transformational structures to carry forward the fight against terror and to help ensure our ultimate success:

- ***Establish and maintain international standards of accountability.*** States that have sovereign rights also have sovereign responsibilities, including the responsibility to combat terrorism. The international community has developed a compelling body of international obligations relating to counterterrorism. Twelve universal conventions and protocols in force against terrorism have been developed under the auspices of the United Nations as well as various U.N. Security Council Resolutions related to combating terror. These include UNSCR 1373, which imposes binding obligations on all states to suppress and prevent terrorist financing, improve their border controls, enhance information sharing and law enforcement cooperation, suppress the recruitment of terrorists, and deny them sanctuary.

  The Group of Eight (G-8) along with other multilateral and regional bodies also have been instrumental in developing landmark counterterrorism standards and best practices that have been adopted by international standard-setting organizations. But our obligations are not static. We will collaborate with our partners to update and tailor international obligations to meet the evolving nature of the terrorist enemies and threats we face. We also will work to ensure that each country is both willing and able to meet its counterterrorist responsibilities. Finally, we will not just continually monitor whether we and the community of nations are meeting these standards but will evaluate if we are achieving results both individually and collectively.

- ***Strengthen coalitions and partnerships.*** Since September 11, most of our important successes against al-Qaida and other terrorist organizations have been made possible through effective partnerships. Continued success depends on the actions of a powerful coalition of nations maintaining a united front against terror. Multilateral groups such as the International Maritime Organization and the International Civil Aviation Organization, as well as regional organizations such as the Asia-Pacific Economic Cooperation, the Organization of American States, NATO, the European Union, the African Union, and the Association of South East Asia Nations, among others, are essential elements of this front.

  We will ensure that such international cooperation is an enduring feature of the long war we will fight. We will continue to leverage the comparative advantage of these institutions and organizations – drawing on what each does best in counterterrorism, from setting standards to developing regional strategies to providing forums for training and education. Indeed, a significant part of this effort includes expanding partnership capacity. We are building the capacity of foreign partners in all areas of counterterrorism activities, including strengthening their ability to conduct law enforcement, intelligence, and military counterterrorism operations. Through the provision of training, equipment, and other assistance, the United States, along with a coalition of willing and able states and organizations, will enhance the ability of partners across the globe to attack and defeat terrorists, deny them funding and freedom of movement, secure their critical infrastructures, and deny terrorists access to WMD and safehavens. Ultimately, it will be essential for our partners to come together to facilitate appropriate international, regional, and local solutions to the challenges of terrorism.

- ***Enhance government architecture and interagency collaboration.*** In the aftermath of September 11, we have enhanced our counterterrorism architecture and interagency collaboration by setting clear national priorities and transforming the government to achieve those priorities. We have established the Department of Homeland Security, bringing under one authority 22 Federal entities with vital roles to play in preventing terrorist attacks within the Homeland, reducing America's vulnerability to terrorism, and minimizing the damage and facilitating the recovery from attacks that do occur. We have reorganized the Intelligence Community. The Director of National Intelligence (DNI) was created to better integrate the efforts of the Community into a more unified, coordinated, and effective whole. The DNI also launched a new Open Source Center to coordinate open source intelligence and ensure this information is integrated into Intelligence Community products.

In addition, a National Counterterrorism Center (NCTC) was established to serve as a multi-agency center analyzing and integrating all intelligence pertaining to terrorism, including threats to U.S. interests at home and abroad. NCTC also is responsible for developing, implementing, and assessing the effectiveness of strategic operational planning efforts to achieve counterterrorism objectives. We similarly established a National Counterproliferation Center to manage and coordinate planning and activities in those areas.

The transformation extends to the Federal Bureau of Investigation, which, with the help of legislation such as the USA PATRIOT Act, is now more fully integrated with the Intelligence Community, has refocused its efforts on preventing terrorism, and has been provided important tools to pursue this mission. CIA also has transformed to fulfill its role to provide overall direction for and coordination of overseas human intelligence operations of Intelligence Community elements. In addition, the Department of the Treasury created the Office of Terrorism and Financial Intelligence to arm ourselves for the long term with the intelligence and tools to undercut the financial underpinnings of terrorism around the world.

The Department of Defense also is preparing to meet a wider range of asymmetric challenges by restructuring its capabilities, rearranging its global posture, and adapting its forces to be better positioned to fight the War on Terror. This includes significantly expanding Special Operations Forces, increasing the capabilities of its general purpose forces to conduct irregular warfare operations, and initiating the largest rearrangement of its global force posture since the end of World War II.

The Department of State is implementing a new framework for foreign assistance to establish more integrated and coherent strategic direction and tactical plans to meet our current and long-term challenges, including terrorism. The State Department also is repositioning its domestic and overseas staff to better promote America's policies and interests and have more direct local and regional impact. This transformational diplomacy positions State to work with partners around the world to build and sustain democratic, well-governed states that will respond to the needs of their people and conduct themselves responsibly in the international system.

We will sustain the transformation already under way in these and other departments and agencies. Moreover, we will continue to build and strengthen a unified team across the counterterrorism community, and a key component of this effort will be fostering "jointness." Where practicable, we will increase interagency and intergovernmental assignments for personnel in counterterrorism-related positions. This will help to break down organizational stovepipes and advance the exchange of ideas and practices for more effective counterterrorism efforts.

- *Foster intellectual and human capital.* To better prepare ourselves for a generational struggle against terrorism and the extremist ideologies fueling it, we will create an expert community of counterterrorism professionals. We will continue to establish more systematic programs for the development and education of current professionals in counterterrorism-related fields. We will substantively expand our existing programs with curricula that includes not only training in counterterrorism policies, plans and planning, strategies, and legal authorities, but continuing education in appropriate area studies, religious philosophies, and languages. We also will ensure that personnel throughout all levels of government and in all fields related to combating terror are invited to participate.

Yet such development and education programs must not be restricted to current counterterrorism personnel. We will support multidisciplinary studies throughout our educational system to build a knowledgeable pool of counterterrorism recruits for the future. The recent National Security Language Initiative is an essential step forward. It will help to expand U.S. foreign language education beginning in early childhood and continuing throughout formal schooling and into the workforce. Our efforts to foster intellectual and human capital also will extend beyond our borders – to academic and non-governmental forums with our international partners to discuss and enhance our knowledge about the critical counterterrorism challenges we confront.

In the War on Terror, there is also a need for all elements of our Nation – from Federal, State, and local governments to the private sector to local communities and individual citizens – to help create and share responsibilities in a Culture of Preparedness. This Culture of Preparedness, which applies to all catastrophes and all hazards, natural or man-made, rests on four principles: a shared acknowledgement of the certainty of future catastrophes and that creating a prepared Nation will be a continuing challenge; the importance of initiative and accountability at all levels of society; the role of citizen and community preparedness; and finally, the roles of each level of government and the private sector in creating a prepared Nation. Built upon a foundation of partnerships, common goals, and shared responsibility, the creation of a Culture of Preparedness will be among our most profound and enduring transformations in the broader effort to protect and defend the Homeland.

Conclusion

Since the September 11 attacks, America is safer, but we are not yet safe. We have done much to degrade al-Qaida and its affiliates and to undercut the perceived legitimacy of terrorism. Our Muslim partners are speaking out against those who seek to use their religion to justify violence and a totalitarian vision of the world. We have significantly expanded our counterterrorism coalition, transforming old adversaries into new and vital partners in the War on Terror. We have liberated more than 50 million Afghans and Iraqis from despotism, terrorism, and oppression, permitting the first free elections in recorded history for either nation. In addition, we have transformed our governmental institutions and framework to wage a generational struggle. There will continue to be challenges ahead, but along with our partners, we will attack terrorism and its ideology, and bring hope and freedom to the people of the world. This is how we will win the War on Terror.

Printed in the USA
CPSIA information can be obtained
at www.ICGtesting.com
JSHW052020140824
68134JS00027B/2566

9 781600 375835